Sing His Praise!

A Case for A Cappella
Music as Worship Today

Sing His Praise!

A Case for A Cappella Music as Worship Today

by
Rubel Shelly

20th Century Christian
Nashville, Tennessee

Table of Contents

Reopening an Old Wound?

One man's reflection on his spiritual background includes the following too-serious-to-be-funny comments:

> We were 'exclusive' Brethren, a branch that believed in keeping itself pure of false doctrine by avoiding association with the impure. ... [W]e made sure that any who fellowshiped with us were straight on all the details of the Faith, as set forth by the first Brethren who left the Anglican Church in 1865 to worship on the basis of correct principles....
>
> Unfortunately, once free of the worldly Anglicans, these firebrands were not content to worship in peace but turned their guns on each other. Scholarly to the core and perfect literalists every one, they set to arguing over points that, to any outsider, would have seemed very minor indeed but which

to them were crucial to the Faith, including the question: if Believer *A* is associated with Believer *B* who has somehow associated himself with *C* who holds a False Doctrine, must *D* break off association with *A*, even though *A* does not hold the Doctrine, to avoid the taint?

The correct answer is: Yes. Some Brethren, however, felt that *D* should only speak with *A* and urge him to break off with *B*. The Brethren who felt otherwise promptly broke off with them. This was the Bedford Question, one of several controversies that, inside of two years, split the Brethren into three branches.

Once having tasted the pleasure of being Correct and defending True Doctrine, they kept right on and broke up at every opportunity, until, by the time I came along, there were dozens of tiny Brethren groups, none of which were speaking to any of the others.[1]

Garrison Keillor, the man who wrote the paragraphs quoted above, is an insightful American humorist who has found a place in the hearts of many of us. First as host of public radio's most popular program, "A Prairie Home Companion," and then as a best-selling author, he has demonstrated an ability to communicate with the masses in this country. His humor is in the tradition of Twain but avoids the acid which is

---

[1]Garrison Keillor, *Lake Wobegon Days* (New York: Viking Penguin Inc., 1985), pp. 105-106).

often found in the latter. A great deal of his work reflects spiritual values related to his own background.

Even more interesting is that he has a connection with the ideal of restoration through his upbringing in the Plymouth Brethren. The Brethren movement began in the early nineteenth century in England. Rejecting all creeds and accepting the Bible alone as their guide in religion, they stressed simplicity in worship and unswerving commitment to the propagation of the truth.

As so often happens, however, commitment to truth frequently degenerated to infighting and unhappy divisions within their ranks. As a humorist, Keillor points to the foibles of his own religious heritage. Representing his past via a fictional town called Lake Wobegon and his spiritual heritage within a church he identifies as the Sanctified Brethren, he dared to poke fun at something very serious. Though some probably regard his words as sacrilegious, we might do well to remember that Jesus used similar humor in talking about specks and planks in people's eyes.

When I read Keillor's thinly veiled description of his personal past as presented in his mythical community of Lake Wobegon, I could not avoid thinking about my own experience within a restorationist heritage. Growing up within the historical framework of a unity movement, I learned and lived with division. I was even comfortable with it, for strict separation creates a strong sense of identity with those few like oneself and an equally strong sense of security. The sense of identity and security which comes of the experience is surely also a type of anesthetic to protect one against the pain of isolation.

Purity and Unity: A Tension

In my own understanding of the Word of God, love of truth and its faithful practice must take precedence over unity with another person. A union created by the compromise of conviction could never be blessed by a Holy God.

The fundamental question of the Christian religion is "What do you think of the Christ?" All of Scripture is focused on Jesus of Nazareth and is designed to lead to faith in him. Diversities of belief concerning the person and work of Jesus do not result from the God-breathed Scripture but from human philosophy. To think that there could be a united church built on a confusion of views about him (i.e., a mythical Christ as well as the divine Christ) is preposterous. If one cannot affirm that Jesus Christ is the Son of God, he has neither part nor lot in the spiritual body of Christ. The heresy of the ecumenical movement has been its attempt to bring under the same umbrella people who embrace different Christs. It was doomed to failure from the start because of its disregard of truth. While unity and harmony are desirable, they cannot be purchased at the expense of the cardinal tenets of Christian faith.

Yet the oneness of those who believe in Jesus is itself a truth of the Scripture which must be maintained alongside the personal convictions one may hold on a variety of issues other than the foundation doctrines of Christianity. While the unity of those who hold conflicting views of the deity of Christ is an impossibility, it should not be impossible for those who have not only confessed his deity but also put him on in baptism to maintain their unity in the face of lesser differences. Must we have different churches around every doctrinal position which is contested among Christians?

Union by a process of "agreeing to disagree" on the fundamental doctrines of Christian faith is unworthy of people who love the God who is Truth in his very nature. Yet perpetual division over lesser points of theology and church ministry by a process of refusing to allow disagreement on any issue at all is equally unworthy.

Thus a tension is created between the apparently incompatible goals of *doctrinal and behavioral purity* on the one hand and *the unity of the church* on the other. Surely the incompatibility of these goals is only apparent rather than real, for both are rooted in clear biblical statements.

Yes, some of the issues which fragment brethren are surely viewed as minor indeed by outsiders. But no issue can be minor to one who lives within a set of circumstances which dictates that one must have a "position." Even the refusal to take a position is itself a position subject to criticism.

Those who are made bitter and cynical by the tension usually leave the tradition altogether. Others who are frustrated but nevertheless manage to avoid bitterness may simply become marginal to the movement and lose their impetus to personal involvement. Still another group is determined to keep fighting it out on every conceivable front without once stopping to realize that their primary contribution is to the bitterness and apathy of the first two groups.

An alternative position is to plead for an ongoing pursuit of *both* unity and purity. Distrust and suspicion must give way to respect; marking out and defending territory must yield to honest inquiry; unity must be understood not as organic bondedness built on conformity but as spiritual oneness in Christ which is based on the divine work of redemption; necessary agreement on the fundamentals of Christian faith must not be confused with allowable diversity on matters of personal faith.

And what of divisions which already exist? The easy path is to accept them without feeling any obligation to heal old wounds. One may assume the rightness of the position he holds and project ignorance and/or dishonesty onto all those who are of a different mind. Returning to Keillor, it is disconcertingly familiar to hear him say:

Patching up was not a Brethren talent. As my Grandpa once said of the Johnson Brethren, 'Anytime they want to come to us and admit their mistake, we're perfectly happy to sit and listen to them and then come to a decision about accepting them back.'[2]

The Issue at Hand: Music

This little book will treat a topic which has been of major importance to a relatively small segment of the American religious community in recent times. The issue of *use versus non-use of instrumental music as Christian worship* is considered trivial by the mainstream evangelical community.[3] It has not always been so, however, and some of the history of controversy over the introduction of musical instruments into various Protestant groups will be traced later in Chapter Four.

Churches of Christ generally stand opposed

---

[2]Ibid., p. 107n.

[3]I consistently speak of instrumental music *as* worship throughout this volume rather than instrumental music *in* worship. I do not consider worship a self-contained unit which can be conveniently proscribed as to time and place. The offering of a psalm, hymn, or spiritual song *as worship* – whether in a church assembly, while riding down the highway in an automobile, in the shower, or at

to musical instruments as worship. There are certain parts of the country, however, where telephone book listings distinguish "Church of Christ – instrumental" from "Church of Christ – a cappella" or "Church of Christ – non-instrumental."

A Roman Catholic writer taking note of this position of opposition to musical instruments as worship among us has done a better-than-average job of accounting for it.

> Their favorite motto, coined by an early 19th-century preacher – 'Where the scriptures speak, we speak; where the scriptures are silent, we are silent' -has led them into polemical battle against all other Christians, Protestant and Catholic. For example, the use of 'mechanical music' in worship has been denounced as evidence of apostasy for more than a century. Obviously the scriptures do not speak of pianos and pipe organs.[4]

---

[4]William J. Whalen, "The Churches of Christ," *U. S. Catholic* 41 (February 1976): 36.

---

summer camp – seems to be the real issue. The view that corporate worship in a church building proceeds in a fundamentally different way and according to fundamentally different principles is untenable in my view. Whatever can be justified as worship for the individual or small group can be justified for the larger group. More detailed discussion of the nature of worship will follow in the primary text of this book.

Neighbors who visit our services for the first time are frequently curious enough about the absence of musical instruments to ask about it. Some ask: "Do you people just not like music?" Others inquire: "Can't you afford to buy an organ for your church?" And surely there are some who believe that we are just a bunch of cranky folks who like to be different from everybody else.

Of course, there are many other issues of larger consequence which separate people within churches of Christ – whether a cappella or instrumental – from Catholics and Protestants around them. A basic attitude toward the all-sufficiency of Scripture and the consequent repudiation of creedal statements or ecclesiastical authority as represented by the papacy or denominational conventions lies at the root of that fundamental posture of separation.

Even among those who share the commitment to Scripture as the only authority in religion, there are differing approaches to the interpretation of the Bible. There is a "strict-interpretation hermeneutic" that some of us adopt which commits us to rejecting things which do not have biblical (or, even more specifically, New Testament) authorization. A "loose-interpretation hermeneutic" allows others to contend that individual believers and local churches have the right to use their own judgment on all issues not explicitly legislated in the New Testament. On the former view, the lack of either a command for or precedent of instrumental music in the pages of the New Testament precludes its use by those who would follow the Scripture faithfully; on the latter view, the fact that the New Testament says nothing of instrumental music in Christian worship means that its use or non-use is a matter of judgment.

A 100-man "Restoration Summit" was conducted on the campus of Ozark Bible College in Joplin, Missouri, August 7-9, 1984. It brought together two groups of believers from the instrumental and non-instrumental wings of the American Restoration Movement to discuss the existing division between the two groups. Other meetings and discussions of a similar nature have followed at irregular intervals.

Such meetings have been misrepresented by a few as "merger talks" between the two groups.

Since neither group has an ecclesiastic organization that allows any person or group to speak for it, merger discussions would be impossible. Since both groups are congregationally self-governing, no one participating in the meetings ever had notions of a modern "ecumenical merger." Each man present represented only his personal views on any topic discussed and never presumed to speak for anyone other than himself.

With the highest possible regard for the Word of God and its final authority in all spiritual matters, those participating in these discussions have tried to get a clearer perspective on things dividing us. Does the silence of the Bible on a given item (e.g., instruments as worship) give one liberty in that regard or establish an exclusionary principle which prohibits the use of human judgment? This question is an issue in biblical interpretation which is both larger than and older than the American Restoration Movement.

The fellowships of believers known as Churches of Christ, Independent Christian Churches, or Conservative Christian Churches are more notable for the similarities between them than for their differences.[5] Congregational autonomy, elders and deacons in each local body, respect for the infallibility of Scripture, focus on the atoning death of Jesus, repentance and baptism as the visible evidences/ expressions of saving faith, weekly observance of the Lord's Supper – these are the tenets of faith one expects to find in seeking to identify the New Testament church. There are also shared practical concerns for making local congregations warm and dynamic fellowships of believers and focal points for effective evangelism. Both groups wrestle with the occasional extremist on the right (i.e., legalism) or left (i.e., liberalism) who threatens the peaceful functioning of the church.

---

[5]Many among the a cappella congregations seem not to have made a clear distinction between the Disciples of Christ denomination and the brotherhood of Conservative Christian Churches. During the past half century, the Christian Church (Disciples of Christ) has gone to the extreme left of the theological spectrum. Liberal theology and immersion in the ecumenical movement have driven a deep wedge between them and the rest of us who have historical roots in the American Restoration Movement. Those of us who do not use instrumental music in worship settings sometimes use "Christian Church" when referring to both the Disciples of Christ and Independent Christian Churches.

It is simply incorrect for those with non-instrument convictions to say (as I have!) that the use of instrumental music among those with a different conviction in the Independent Christian Churches stems from a lack of respect for the authority of Scripture. The use or non-use of instrumental music in worship relates to a hermeneutical method (i.e., how to interpret the so-called "silence" of Scripture) rather than a difference of view concerning the sufficiency and authority of the Bible.

Why Write This Book?

My purpose in writing this book relates directly to the series of events just related. As discussions continue between estranged groups of Christians who are tied together historically by the American Restoration Movement, the specific topics which divide us must be discussed. The most productive forum for doing so is not in heated verbal debates of the sort that originally deepened our division but through printed media. Positions can be articulated with calm deliberation. Readers can follow, weigh, and study for themselves.

From one perspective, it might be chided as the reopening of an old wound. From the perspective of my intention, however, this book is not designed to serve any such negative end. Whether intention and result conform, only time will reveal.

With better understanding of brethren who hold a different position than mine on instrumental music as worship, I have better hope of addressing the issues of real concern to them and answering their questions and/or objections appropriate to my position. Others can present the case for a cappella music in worship as well or better than I can in this book, but none will do so with more brotherly concern for those who hold a differing view. Since we will both be judged by Christ at the Last Day, it is no part of my obligation or desire to judge those who differ with me – nor is it my concern to be judged by them.

Salvation for any one of us will be by grace and not by virtue of perfect theology or character. This is not to say, however, that issues of this sort are therefore reduced to meaningless insignificance. If I did not believe the position to be set forth in this book to be correct and its opposite wrong, I would not bother to write. But I will not insult either the intelligence or integrity of those who hold a contrary position. My obligation is to learn and practice and teach truth. It is not my task to pronounce anathemas but to seek and teach truth.

Even among congregations which do not use the instrument, there is a need to study this topic. It alarms me that I have met or read from brethren who hold membership in a cappella congregations yet do not feel instrumental music to be a violation of Scripture but a mere matter of taste or opinion. A rather large number of young adults I have known through my experience as a teacher in two Christian colleges have admitted to me that they really do not understand why opposition to the use of instruments as worship is part of our heritage.

In some situations it may be that the lack of musical instruments in worship is not so much due to conviction as tradition. It is tragic to consider the possibility that some Christians do not know why they subscribe to the religious practices in which they participate. They may tell their acquaintances "*We* believe such and such about baptism" or "*We* believe this about

22

the worship of the church" and be totally unable to justify their "beliefs" (?) when questioned. They refer the questioner to the preacher. Is this not a type of creedalism? Is it not an admission that these people have made an uncritical commitment to doctrines they do not understand?

Milton, in his *Areopagitica,* wrote: "A man may be a heretic in the truth; and if he believe things only because his pastor says so, or the assembly so determine, without knowing other reason, though his belief be true, yet the very truth he holds becomes his heresy." The value of any belief – even a true one – is prostituted by virtue of the fact that one has derived it not from personal inquiry but from loyalty to a certain religious party or charming teacher.

Perhaps each of us should take inventory of his or her beliefs. How many things do you believe because "My church teaches ... "? Is your view on faith, baptism, the Lord's Supper, church organization, a cappella music, and Christian security due to personal study of Scripture or what you have always heard from the pulpit? If one's views derive from the latter rather than the former, he is sectarian and heretical.

Churches of Christ claim to be undenominational and nonsectarian. To the degree that we exalt Christ through faithfulness to the Word of God, the claim is legitimate. To the degree that we hold positions (even true ones!) because a trusted person, paper, or institution said it, we are unfaithful to our calling.

Against the danger of holding an unquestioned view on any topic of relevance to our personal lives, spiritual integrity should move us to study and think for ourselves.

Conclusion

The goal of this book, then, is to articulate a case for a cappella music as the type of musical praise appropriate to the worship of the people of God in such a way as to allow people to have access to data for personal reflection. My hope is that some who are of my tradition will be provided the basis for intelligent personal conviction on the matter from reading it and that the general position of commitment to a cappella music will be strengthened among brethren from my own background. I hope some of a contrary view will be convinced to change their mind and practice by reading.

At the very least, perhaps some who know the non-instrument position only through caricature and misrepresentation will understand why some of us hold this view with sincere conviction –even if their own views remain unaltered.

The Authority Question

The issue of central significance with regard to the use or non-use of instrumentation with Christian praise of God in song is respect for the authority of the Word of God and one's understanding of how biblical authority is to be derived and followed.

There are some in the religious world who have no sense of need about establishing biblical authority for their beliefs and practices. They are very open and bold about their disdain for the notion of doing so. They regard Christianity as an evolutionary phenomenon and have no qualms about leaving behind "crude, early dogma" in order to adopt positions which they think are more in keeping with an enlightened time. Typical of such a mindset is the following statement from a professor of theology at Harvard Divinity School:

> Though we may recognize and be grateful for its contributions to our culture, the Bible no longer has unique authority for Western man. It has become a great but archaic monument in our midst. It is a reminder of where we once were – but no longer are. It contains glorious literature, important historical documents, exalted ethical teachings, but it is no longer the word of God (if there is a God) to man.[1]

Someone with this attitude toward the authority of the Bible could never take the issue of this little book seriously. He feels no obligation to be guided by Scripture in his beliefs or practices. Whatever he chooses to do is what he will do – regardless of any biblical command or statement relevant to it. This is an extreme known as *theological liberalism*. This position has cut itself off from any obligation to operate within the parameters established by the Word of God.

Those of us with a background within the

---

[1]Gordon D. Kaufman, "What Shall We Do With the Bible?" *Interpretation* 25 (January 1971): 96.

historical tradition known as the American Restoration Movement know very little about theological liberalism. In fact, we hardly know how to use the term correctly. It is not uncommon for us to hear people branded as "liberals" for such things as using modern-speech translations of the Bible. A true liberal is someone who denies the inspiration and authority of the Bible. It is neither correct nor honest to stick that label on someone who holds to biblical infallibility but with whom you may disagree on a point of interpretation.

One stream of the American Restoration Movement has moved headlong in the direction of liberalism. The leadership of the Disciples of Christ has positioned itself well to the left on the theological spectrum. Many members of the Disciples and not a few local church leaders are considerably more conservative than the group's national leadership, however, and are very unhappy about their denomination's stance.

It would be difficult, if not impossible, to elicit concern for establishing biblical authority for instrumental music among anyone in the Disciples of Christ national leadership.

The discussion of instrumental music to take

place in this book will be of primary interest to people in the Conservative Christian Churches and Churches of Christ. Both groups are theologically conservative. It would be only rarely that someone in a position of leadership within either of these fellowships would challenge the inspiration (i.e., infallibility) and authority of the Bible. Our differences would be over the interpretation of specific passages rather than over the general issue of biblical authority.

More specifically still, the differences of interpretation tend to center on the issue of how the two estranged groups understand what has come to be called the "silence of Scripture." Suppose there is a topic such as instrumental music in worship where the New Testament neither requires nor prohibits by explicit statement. What rights do we have? Is the silence of the Word of God on the subject to be interpreted as divine liberty to do as we see fit within the general framework of the New Testament? Some hold this view. Or is the silence of the New Testament to be understood as a lack of authority and thus deemed to exclude actions under certain conditions? Others of us hold this view.

In this chapter an attempt will be made to set

forth a consistent and scripturally derived understanding of divine authority and how it relates to this topic of musical praise.

The Authority Principle

A New Testament teaching which is fundamental to the principle of restoration is that *all things believed, taught, and/or practiced in the Christian religion must have divine authority.* These words from Paul state the principle: "And whatever you do, whether in word or deed, do it all in the name of the Lord Jesus, giving thanks to God the Father through him" (Col. 3:17). To do a thing "in the name of the Lord Jesus" is to do it in light of and in harmony with the revelation of his will for mankind. The full authority of God is inherent in the very words of Holy Scripture (cf. Matt. 18:18; 1 Cor. 14:37; 1 Thess. 2:13), and Scripture furnishes one completely for the service of God (2 Tim. 3:17).

Again, Christ's faithful disciples seek always to "live by faith, not by sight" (2 Cor. 5:7). To live by faith is to direct one's ways by the revealed will of God, as opposed to relying on the limited insights one can have into the mind of

God through his own reflections and deductions. Faith comes to us by hearing the message of the Word of God (Rom. 10:17). If there is no authority from the message of Christ for a given doctrine or practice, that doctrine or practice cannot be "from faith" and is therefore sinful (cf. Rom. 14:23).

These are very general principles which would need to be argued in great detail with some in the larger Protestant world but which are common to those who share a background within the American Restoration Movement. Alexander Campbell, for example, rejected sprinkling as an acceptable form of baptism on the ground of God's failure to authorize its use. In his debates with Walker, McCalla, and Rice, he never claimed that Scripture condemned sprinkling. He did not make the unjustified claim that a statement could be produced from the New Testament forbidding affusion.

In their consistent and emphatic rejection of sprinkling for baptism, the early restoration leaders pointed to the absence of either a New Testament command for sprinkling or data in Scripture or early church history to show that the primitive body of Christ used sprinkling.

From this biblical "silence," they inferred that immersion alone had divine authority and subsequently opposed affusion.

The opposition of many within the restoration tradition to instrumental music as worship is based on the same form of reasoning. I do not claim to be able to produce an explicit prohibition of such music from the New Testament. There is neither a command for instrumental accompaniment to Christian musical praise nor data in Scripture or early church history to show that the primitive body of Christ used it. From this "silence" it is inferred that singing alone has divine authority and that instrumental accompaniment to singing is outside the parameters of biblical authority available to us.

In passing, it should be noted that those of us who do not use instrumental music are generally assumed to bear the burden of proof in justifying such a position. As a matter of fact, we have generally acted somewhat defensively by being quick to offer arguments for its non-use. But the burden of proof logically belongs to those who engage in the practice. By analogy, I have no rational obligation to justify my non-affusionist practices by making a case against sprinkling. Only if Scripture somehow mandated sprinkling would I bear the burden of proof for my failure to do so. Since I am an immersionist, my only burden of proof is to that practice. Similarly I have no rational obligaton to justify my non-instrument position by making a case against pianos and organs in Christian worship. Only if Scripture somehow mandated instruments would I bear the obligation for my a cappella worship. Since I worship God with vocal praise, my only obligation is to produce authority for that practice.

It would certainly be a mistake to suppose that anything not expressly forbidden in Scripture is therefore divinely authorized.

If it were the case that anything not expressly forbidden in the New Testament is permissible in the Christian religion, then we could not only use pianos to accompany our singing but beads to aid our prayers, crucifixes to focus our devotion, and hashish to enhance our sensitivity. We could also initiate an organizational network similar to that which has been protested so strongly in Catholicism or begin financing church projects with bingo games (where legal) on Tuesday evenings. Not one of these things is explicitly forbidden in the New Testament, and no one who denies the legitimacy of the authority principle as outlined above can consistently argue against any of them.

> This principle [of allowing anything not specifically forbidden], pushed to its ultimate conclusion, will admit anything men may desire into the service of God, so that every man again may become a law unto himself. If the Gospel is to be preached and the church preserved in anything like their pristine purity, such a principle as this is absolutely inadmissible.[2]

It would also be a mistake to think that silence is never concessive, for everyone understands it so in certain instances. For example, there is no command for Christians to purchase property, build church buildings, and appoint real estate trustees. Neither is there any precedent in the New Testament which can be identified where such practices were followed by the earliest Christians. Similar observations could be made about communion ware, electric lights, air conditioning, public address systems, pews, four-part harmony, song books, or tuning forks.

---

[2]Olan Hicks in the "Introduction" to Homer Hailey, *Attitudes and Consequences in the Restoration Movement* (Rosemead, CA: Old Paths Book Club, 1952), p. 7.

The Old Testament command to sing praise unto God clearly did not exclude instrumental music as worship. There seems to be no such intent in the command. Furthermore, the additional Old Testament references which either command or illustrate the use of instruments as worship preclude understanding its authorization of singing as having exclusionary force. On the other hand, the New Testament command about singing God's praise appears to be different from the one in the Old Testament. Unlike the Old Testament, there is a total absence (i.e., silence) of commands for or illustration of the use of instruments as worship. Let me repeat the point made earlier: I do not oppose instrumental music as worship because it is prohibited by the command to sing but because of the absence of any supplemental authority to play instruments as worship. Recall the parallel case of immersion and sprinkling: I do not oppose sprinkling as baptism because it is prohibited by the command to immerse but because of the absence of any supplemental authority to practice affusion.

At times one suspects that what one allows and prohibits is due more to taste and temperament than to any clearly articulated doctrine of biblical authority. Whether that is so or not, responsible Christians who are concerned about biblical interpretation must try to find a hermeneutic which is sound and constructive. A conscientious effort must be made to avoid having each of us become a law to himself.

From the study of Scripture itself, it seems clear that silence must in some instances be understood as having exclusionary force. Take the argument from the book of Hebrews concerning Christ's priesthood as a case in point. In the course of an argument showing that a change of covenants had taken place in the scheme of redemption, great emphasis is placed on an argument from silence.

That the old covenant given through Moses was temporary and destined to be replaced by a new one is held by the writer of Hebrews to be implied in anointing of Jesus to be a priest after the order óf Melchizedek. Thus he writes:

> If perfection could have been attained through the Levitical priesthood (for on the basis of it the law was given to the people), why was there still need for another priest to come – one like Melchizedek, not like Aaron? For when there is a change of the priesthood, there must also be a change of

the law. He of whom these things are said belonged to a different tribe, and no one from that tribe has ever served at the altar. For it is clear that our Lord descended from Judah, and in regard to that tribe Moses said nothing about priests (Heb. 7:11-14).

There is no explicit prohibition of taking priests from the tribe of Judah in the Old Testament. What is contained in the Law of Moses is authorization for appointing priests from the tribe of Levi. If there had been supplemental legislation authorizing priests from other tribes, the situation would have been other than the writer of Hebrews – and all other students of the Old Testament – interpreted it to be. It was the lack of other commands or examples of non-Levitical priests which made the exclusionary force of the command about priests from Levi obvious.

A command, law, or other authoritative statement authorizes only what it authorizes and does not have to exclude all other alternatives by means of detailed prohibitions. A physician's prescription for penicillin does not have to forbid the pharmacist from either substituting or adding other antibiotics; it authorizes only what is identified. A customer's order for item

#4ZH9753 does not have to exclude every other item in the mail-order catalog he is using by means of listing them; it authorizes only what is named on the order blank.

The authority principle works this way generally. We understand it in relation to physicians' prescriptions and customers' orders but sometimes fail to realize that it applies to spiritual matters as well. When God authorizes through his Word, he has authorized only that which has been identified and does not have to exclude all other possibilities with a series of injunctions.

It is probably incorrect to refer to this sort of thing as an "argument from silence." God was hardly silent about the Old Testament priesthood. He authorized priests to be selected from the descendants of Levi. His failure to name Judah or any of the other tribes simply meant that the priesthood was limited to the tribe of Levi. The exclusionary force of the command was clear in context.

As a matter of common sense, one can understand that every form of authorization is more or less specific, has certain inclusive and exclusive features, and may have to be studied carefully as to all its implications. Think first of one of the analogies used above and then reason back to what this means about our understanding of Scripture.

Let us suppose that a physician is working in a third-world country, trying to bring primary medical care to a group of people. It is altogether conceivable that he might issue an appeal to fellow physicians, pharmacists, or drug companies: "Please send me whatever antibiotics you can spare." The request is quite broad, yet it has its exclusive features. There are many different antibiotics on the market. The appeal includes penicillin but is not limited to it. It also includes antibiotics of other types because of its broad wording. While it is broad in regard to all antibiotics, it is nevertheless exclusive in relation to tranquilizers, digitalis, antacids, and scores of other non-antibiotic medications.

Suppose now that our physician friend is practicing medicine in New York City. Instead of issuing a general appeal for antibiotics, let us assume that he writes a prescription for a specific patient which calls for 250 mg. of tetracycline to be taken three times a day. This is a much more specific situation than the first one envisioned. All antibiotics other than the one named are ruled out; all other dosages are eliminated. Yet there is also some degree of breadth left to it. Several different drug companies manufacture specific brands of this medication, and the pharmacist may exercise his judgment in picking the specific capsules from his shelf which the patient will take home with him.

Let's take it one step further, however, and suppose that the physician prescribes not only a specific medication and dosage but also identifies a brand name. The prescription is now very specific and places a pharmacist within clearly defined limits.

When Alexander Campbell and others rejected sprinkling as an acceptable form of baptism, they did so on the basis of reasoning which follows the pattern illustrated above. He observed that the New Testament did not contain a broad command such as "perform a religious ceremony with water in order to admit men into the body of Christ." If that had been the biblical authorization, any method from full immersion to sprinkling would have satisfied the command. Broad as this command would have been, it would have still had exclusive force. It would have ruled out religious rites which do not involve water as suitable for securing entrance into the church.

Campbell argued that Scripture authorizes a specific action which is denoted by the verb *baptizein*. This verb refers to the action of dipping, submerging, or immersing. Thus it was argued that to speak of pouring or sprinkling as alternate "modes" of baptism was illogical. Since the command to baptize is specific as to the action indicated, it is only that action (i.e., immersion) which has been authorized.

> The exclusion of affusion, therefore, is not based upon the silence of the New Testament on sprinkling but on what God said *do*. The silence of the New Testament and the evidence that sprinkling was not practiced until a later date have a bearing. The fact that baptism was commanded would not exclude sprinkling if there were *another* direct command to do it (*rantizein*). If the New Testament and early church history showed that sprinkling was practiced, then its approval might be shown by precedent or necessary inference. But silence in these two areas coupled with the specific commandment meant that the practice is unscriptural.[3]

Even with a command which is specific as to

---

[3] J. W. Roberts, "Instrumental Music (2)," *Firm Foundation* (1967): 615.

the action of baptism, there remain certain areas of "silence" where our judgment appears to be required. Is immersion to be performed in running or still water? What (if anything) is to be said over the candidate seeking baptism? Should one's baptism be a public ceremony performed before the church or a private affair?

It is precisely this same pattern of reasoning which those of us who argue for a cappella music use in making our case.

If God had authorized Christians to "offer musical praise to God," it would have been our choice to do so by vocal, instrumental, or combined vocal and instrumental music. But the New Testament contains no such general and broad authorization for music of unspecified origin and nature. To the contrary, the musical vocabulary of the New Testament employs words which indicate the specific action of vocal praise. Both the New Testament and early church history point to the exclusive use of vocal music for divine praise and mutual exhortation among Christians. Thus, against the "silence" of New Testament authority for instrumental music as praise to God, it is excluded in the same way that authority for immersion excludes the legitimacy of sprinkling. The absence of any authority for using instruments other than the human heart and voice seems to point to an exclusionary intent in the commands about singing.

With specific authority for vocal music, there still remain areas of "silence" where we use human judgment. Shall we print words and/or music or sing only from memory? Shall we sing in unison or with four-part harmony?

In summary, Scripture authorizes with varying degrees of specificity. When it authorizes an act without stating the precise method of its accomplishment, its "silence" on the particulars of accomplishment is to be understood as concessive to human judgment and initiative consistent with the letter and spirit of the Christian system. When it authorizes a specific activity, its "silence" about related actions narrows one to the activity identified and thereby excludes other methods not authorized elsewhere.

Difficulty in Communication

Those of us who hold such a view have apparently done a poor job of communicating with those who take an opposite view. As it is occasionally reflected to us, it comes back in forms similar to this:

> Quite simply, they urge that every affirmative command of God is also negative; it forbids not only the opposite of what is commanded, but it forbids doing anything that is not commanded to be done.[4]

One who has followed the affirmative case presented already in this chapter should be able to see that a subtle but substantial difference exists in the case argued here and the one represented in this objection.

Take the command about baptism to illustrate the difference. One would hardly be inclined to say it forbids not only its opposite (staying dry?) but also doing anything not commanded to be done. The command to be baptized does not command calling others together to witness the event; it does not command urging others to imitate his example; it does not command changing into dry clothes after the rite; it does not command heating the water in Minnesota during February before the rite, etc.

Pressed to its ultimate, the notion that the

---

[4]Edwin V. Hayden, "An Unbearable Yoke," *Christian Standard* (June 23, 1985): 556.

command to baptize forbids anything not specifically commanded by the word would eliminate faith and repentance. No New Testament command excludes things which are commanded elsewhere in the same document.

No informed person would say that the command to baptize forbids warming the water, changing clothes, or calling others to witness the event. None of these actions alters the nature of the authorized event which is occurring. The command to baptize would not exclude affusion if another passage could be cited from the New Testament to authorize it as an alternative to immersion.

It is not the case that the command to sing "forbids not only the opposite of what is commanded, but it forbids doing anything that is not commanded to be done." The command to sing authorizes printing song books, just as the command to baptize authorizes warming water. It is not necessary to do either, but it may be expedient to do one or both. The command to sing authorizes a leader and a public address system, just as the command to baptize authorizes an immerser and a public address system.

When these brethren say, 'Where the Bible speaks we

speak; and where the Bible is silent we are silent,' they mean, 'Where the Bible commands we must command; and where the Bible commands we must forbid.'[5]

This misses the focus of the controversy over biblical authority by a wide margin. No one has the right to use a biblical command to forbid – if there are other relevant commands or authorizing statements which can be introduced. No one would have the right to use the command to appoint priests from the tribe to Levi to forbid appointing men from Judah to the priesthood – if there were statements in the old covenant authorizing men of Judah to the Aaronic priesthood. No one would have the right to use the command to immerse to forbid sprinkling – if there were statements in the new covenant authorizing affusion. And no one would have the right to use the command to sing to forbid instrumentation – if there were other statements in the New Testament to authorize it.

The fact is, however, that one does not have the right to appoint Aaronic priests from Judah, encourage and practice affusion as baptism, or offer Christian praise to God with instruments

---

[5]Ibid.

in the absence of divine authority in the Word of God.

The correct question is not "Where does Scripture forbid X?" but "Where does the Word of God authorize X?" And there is simply no New Testament authority for instrumental music as sacred praise. There is certainly no command that it be used in either private or public settings of worship. Neither is there any record of its use in the first century, which would authorize it by apostolic precedent.

New Testament authority is for *singing* as the means of musical praise to God in the Christian Age. Such passages as Ephesians 5:19 and Colossians 3:16 call for "speaking," "teaching," "admonishing," "singing," and "making music in your heart." Each of these actions is related to verbal activity, and not one of them can be performed by a mechanical instrument of music.

Nature of Worship

One possible response to all this is to insist that worship is only an emotion and has nothing to do with outward expressions. But if that is true, no *action* (i.e., practice, deed) is subject to regulation as worship. Worship would be entirely a matter of the heart and unrelated to the actions which flow from that heart.

In reply to this view, it should be noted that no biblical passage defines worship as a mere emotion. To the contrary, Scripture requires not only that one's heart be right in worship but that his actions be performed according to the revealed will of God. If the "expression" of the emotion really does not matter, how could one be justified in opposing beads, candles, icons, and the like?

That worship does involve actions as well as emotion can be demonstrated by an examination of the Greek words which are translated "worship" in the New Testament. *Proskyneo* means "(fall down and) worship, do obeisance to, prostrate oneself before, do reverence to, welcome respectfully."[6] *Latreuo* is defined to mean "serve, in our lit. only of the carrying out of

---

[6]Walter Bauer, *A Greek-English Lexicon of the New Testament,* trans William F. Arndt and F. Wilbur Gingrich, 2nd. ed. revised and augmented by F. Wilbur Gingrich and Frederick W. Danker (Chicago: University of Chicago Press, 1979), s.v. *"proskyneo,"* pp. 716-717.

relig. duties, esp. of a cultic nature, by human beings."[7] *Sebomai* means "to reverence, shrink back in fear, worship."[8]

These and other words used in Scripture indicate that worship is concerned not only with pure motives but correct actions. This is why the Savior could quote Isaiah in denouncing certain Pharisees and teachers of the Law and say: "They worship me in vain; their teachings are but rules made by man" (Matt. 15:9). Although rendered "vain" by replacing the divine will with human rules and/or false motives, the fact remained that their involvement in certain reverential acts constituted "worship."

A footnote to the word "worship" (Gk, *proskyneo*) in Matthew 2:2 as translated in the American Standard Version says: "The Greek word denotes an act of reverence whether paid to a creature (see ch. 4.9; 18.26) or to the Creator (see ch. 4.10)." The central concept in all the worship vocabulary of Scripture is service offered to another. The emotion underlying the

---

[7]Ibid., s.v. *"latreuo,"* p. 467.

[8]*New International Dictionary of New Testament Theology,* Vol. 2, 1976 ed, s.v. "Godliness, Piety," by W. Gunther, p. 91.

service is critical, but the service itself constitutes worship when being offered to God.

In the case of the Jewish teachers of Matthew 15, their formal teaching of the Law constituted an activity of worship. When the Word of God is preached by an evangelist or teacher today, it is an act of worship. In the Old Testament, offering sacrifices (cf. Isa. 19:21), playing trumpets and singing (Cf. 2 Chron. 29:25-30), or bowing down before idols (cf. Mic. 5:13) are all identified as worship. The New Testament vocabulary of worship follows this same pattern.

Worship is not merely a feeling but the expression of one's devotion in actions. The critical issue is whether or not one has biblical authority for the actions he offers as divine service. Neither right acts with wrong motives nor wrong acts with right motives constitute pure worship. It is authorized actions offered from hearts with pure motives which constitute the worship our God deserves.

While on the general topic of worship, two other observations are appropriate here.

First, it is not correct to claim "All of life is one's worship to God" or "Worship is everything a Christian does." This rather popular notion of our time stems from a confusion of *service* and *worship*. Whereas all worship is service to God (thus we can speak of a "worship service"), not all service to God is worship. Whereas eating and drinking glorify God as service (cf. 1 Cor. 10:31), eating and drinking (for physical nourishment) are not worshipful acts. Common sense and the following biblical data will demonstrate this difference.

Abraham did not consider his life to be continuous worship. He saddled his donkey, called his servants, cut wood, traveled, made camp, and told his servants, "Stay here with the donkey while I and the boy go over there. We will worship and then we will come back to you" (Gen. 22:5). Worship punctuated a life of continuous commitment to the Lord for Abraham, but he understood that worship was something other than the normal routine of his life. On Sundays, my shower, shave, and breakfast are different in nature from an identifiable experience I share with others and call worship.

This is the pattern for biblical language. After the death of David's illegitimate child by Bathsheba, the text reports: "Then David got up from the ground. After he had washed, put on lotions and changed his clothes, *he went into the house of the Lord and worshiped*. Then he went to his own house, and at his request they served him food, and he ate" (2 Sam. 12:20). Worship begins and ends. It is distinguishable from mourning, bathing, and eating.

The New Testament uses the same language pattern. Luke writes of the Ethiopian whom Philip brought to salvation: "This man had *gone to Jerusalem to worship,* and on his way home was sitting in his chariot reading the book of Isaiah the prophet" (Acts 8:27b-28). Traveling, providing for one's family, visiting the sick, and mowing a sick neighbor's yard are all service to God. They are not worship, however, and it is not characteristic of us to speak of them as such.

Second, the essence of worship is internal rather than external. Having gone to some length to argue above that worship relates to the offering of certain reverential actions to God, that truth must be balanced with a companion truth that nothing external is intrinsically worshipful. Bowing one's knee before Jesus may be worship, but it can also be mockery. For the twelve apostles, it was the former; for the soldiers in

Pilate's court, it was the latter. Unless the internal state is reverential and appropriate to the deed being offered, there is no value as worship to the actions performed.

The New Testament does not teach a sacramental view of worship. Prescribed ceremonies without proper heart involvement is empty. That is why the Lord quoted Isaiah to rebuke those who honor God "with their lips" but "their hearts are far from [God]" (Matt. 15:8).

The factor which makes singing meaningful worship is not merely that it is authorized activity, but that the activity is coming from a reverent, loving, and consecrated heart. It would be a shallow protest to inveigh against corrupting the action (i.e., adding instruments to the musical praise of the church) without also warning against neglecting its very essence (i.e., adoration from a devoted heart).

Since the church is authorized to assemble on the first day of the week and to exhort one another in the Word, there can be no question that we are also authorized to employ psalms, hymns, and spiritual songs in those assemblies. This is true in light of the fact that the earliest Christians were commanded to "speak to one another" (whether individually or corporately) by means of these literary forms.

Whether or not to assemble was not left as an option for the church, thus the forsaking of the assembly is warned against at Hebrews 10:25. The purpose for such assemblies is known to us through biblical and secular history. Worship focused on Christ by means of the Lord's Supper as a memorial to his death and resurrection and also through prayer and teaching. One form of teaching, along with preaching, dialogue, and other means, was the praise of God in song (1 Cor. 14:15-16). If the musical vocabulary of the New Testament and early church history demonstrate that such singing was a cappella in nature, we should adopt the same procedure. If they show it was always accompanied by instrumentation, we should adopt that procedure. If language study and history demonstrate that the use or non-use of instruments was optional, we should not insist on conformity to either procedure to the exclusion of the other.

Conclusion

There is more at stake in the instrumental

music question than the mere presence or absence of a piano in a worship setting. What is at stake is the much larger issue of how one understands biblical authority and the hermeneutic he will use in interpreting the Word of God.

To summarize this chapter, I have tried to explain the approach to Scripture some of us feel compelled to take. Respecting the divine inspiration of the Bible, we attempt to interpret it with a hermeneutic inductively derived from inspired literature. Specifically, I believe that one must have divine authorization for all his beliefs and practices, rather than presume on the "silences" of Scripture to introduce things which are without divine warrant.

Just as the old covenant's specification of priests to be taken from the tribe of Levi prohibited Jesus (who was of the tribe of Judah) from functioning as a priest under that law, I believe the new covenant's specification of vocal music for praise to God and exhortation among saints prohibits the use of instrumental music. This is the same line of reasoning used by those of us who oppose affusion as an acceptable form of baptism. To be sure, immersion does not exclude sprinkling if additional information can be produced which shows it equally acceptable to God. Neither would singing exclude instrumentation if the New Testament provided data showing it was also employed with divine approval in the early church. In the absence of such information, both sprinkling and instrumental music should be abandoned in favor of the biblical practices of immersion and a cappella music.

The critical questions remaining are these: (1) Is the musical vocabulary of the New Testament specific enough to justify the claim that it points to vocal music alone? (2) Does early church history demonstrate that a cappella singing was used exclusively by Christians in its musical praise? (3) What are the present implications of the instrumental music controversy to the divided state of believers within the heritage of the American Restoration Movement?

With singing, prayer, or communion, it is not the act alone which is worship. It is the authorized action accompanied by an involved heart which is true worship. Or, perhaps more correctly still, it is the worshipful and open heart which expresses itself in an authorized action which is true worship.

No Law, No Sin

Another objection which is sometimes made against the authority principle as explained above is this: There is no law against instrumental music, and where there is no law there is no sin. There is nothing in this objection that has not been dealt with in the materials already presented. Thus, a few general observations will be sufficient.

It is again conceded that no explicit statement of prohibition is found in the New Testament regarding instrumental music as worship among Christians. Yet proof has already been offered which shows that a thing need not be specifically condemned in order to be unauthorized. A physician's prescription calling for penicillin does not have to exclude all other antibiotics by name. By specifying penicillin, he implicitly excludes the others. The divine authorization for singing in the New Testament has the same effect. By specifying vocal praise which teaches and admonishes and by simultaneously failing to authorize instruments as praise, the New Testament implicitly excludes instrumental music as worship.

No Corporate Singing in NT

Still another objection to this line of reasoning takes another approach altogether. It seeks to eliminate the controversy over instrumental music in worship by arguing that all the references to singing in the New Testament refer to individual singing and not to corporate worship. The thesis of this position appears to be that congregational singing is itself a matter of choice or expediency rather than divine command. Thus, if congregational singing is itself a matter of expediency rather than mandate, whether such singing is accompanied or unaccompanied must also be viewed as a matter of expediency.

It would be a difficult thing to prove that all the New Testament references to singing are, in fact, non-congregational in nature. In Ephesians 5:19, for example, the singing is clearly being done by people in association with others. Thus the command to "speak to one another" is found. In order for mutual edification to occur by congregational or antiphonal singing, there has to be some sort of corporate entity.

For the sake of the objection at hand, however, let us grant the point that all the New

Testament passages which speak of singing are non-congregational. My objection is not and has never been to instrumental accompaniment to congregational singing as opposed to individual singing. I find no New Testament authority for musical praise in the life of the church today other than vocal praise. Whether congregational or individual, antiphonal or solo, in a large auditorium built for corporate worship or in a jail cell – what form(s) of music has God authorized?

The
Musical
Vocabulary
of the
New Testament

One of the more important investigations relating to the question of instrumental music as praise to God has to do with the musical vocabulary of the Greek New Testament. More specifically, the issue focuses on the words *psallo* (a verb translated "making melody," "make melody," "sing psalms," and "make music" in the KJV, ASV, RSV, and NIV) and *psalmos* (a noun translated "psalm" in our English versions).[1] The point at issue is this: Do these words

---

[1]*Psallo* occurs in Rom. 15:9; 1 Cor. 14:15(2); Eph. 5:19; Jas. 5:13. *Psalmos* is found at Luke 20:42; 24:44; Acts 1:20; 13:33; 1 Cor. 14:26; Eph. 5:19; Col. 3:16.

signify singing with the human voice or do they either require or allow accompaniment by some form of mechanical instrument?

In 1920 O. E. Payne published a book which argued that *psallo* means "to play the harp" in the New Testament and thus authorizes instrumental music.[2] The same argument has been made more recently by brothers such as Tom Burgess and Dwaine Dunning. As to the lexical data pertinent to the words, Burgess insists, "The force of the lexicons ... stands unitedly for songs sung to instrumental accompaniment."[3] Of the noun, Dunning says: "Psalm is an instrumental performance which may be – but does not absolutely require that it be – accompanied by the voice."[4] Of the verb, he writes: "Massive evidence shows that an instrument inheres in *Psallo* exactly and essentially as 'much water' inheres in *baptizo*."[5]

---

[2]O. E. Payne, *Instrumental Music is Scriptural* (Cincinnati: Standard Publishing Co., 1920).

[3]Tom Burgess, *Documents on Instrumental Music* (Portland, OR: Scripture Supply House, 1964), p. 46.

[4]Dwaine Dunning, "Schism by Syllogism," p. 3. (Mimeographed).

[5]Ibid., p. 11.

In this chapter we shall investigate the musical vocabulary of the Greek New Testament with a view toward evaluating claims of the sort just cited. The data will be seen to authorize vocal praise to God through song and provide no authority for mechanical instruments of music.

Please note that no argument is being made to the effect that *psallo* (or any other of the Greek words involved) means "do not play pianos" or inveighs against instruments in general. If Scripture somewhere authorizes instruments as appropriate praise to God by Christians, this word would not preclude their use. The argument being made concerning *psallo* is simply that *it authorizes singing,* and we can do only what is authorized in the New Testament.[6]

---

[6]Some persons miss the significance of this point, but it needs to be clear at the beginning of this discussion of the Greek words in question. Perhaps a reminder about the parallel drawn in the previous chapter between the affusion and the instrument controversies will be helpful. The word *baptizo* does not mean "do not sprinkle water on people." It authorizes immersion but would not rule out sprinkling if the latter action were authorized of God in some way. Restorationists have insisted that our affusionist friends should acknowledge the action involved in the word *baptizo* (i.e., immersion) and not go beyond

The Lexical Data

Our study begins with a simple listing of lexical information on the verb *psallo* from a number of sources.

Newman defines the word: "sing, sing a hymn of praise, sing praise."[7]

The Grimm-Wilke-Thayer lexicon says: "to pluck off, pull out ... to cause to vibrate by touching, to twang ... to touch or strike the chord, to twang the strings of a musical instrument so that they gently vibrate ... and absol. to play on a stringed instrument, to play the harp, etc. ... Sept. for *nagan* and much oftener for *zamar;* to sing to the music of the harp; in the N.T. to sing a hymn, to celebrate the praises of God in song, Jas. v. 13."[8]

---

[7]Barclay M. Newman, Jr., *A Concise Greek-English Dictionary of the New Testament,* 1971 ed., s.v. "*psallo.*"

[8]C. G. Wilke and C. L. Wilibald Grimm, *Greek-English Lexicon of the New Testament,* trans. Joseph Henry Thayer, 1889 ed., s.v. "*psallo.*"

---

what it authorizes to add a second form of initiation ritual to the Christian religion. Similarly, those of us who plead for a cappella music insist that people should acknowledge the action involved in *psallo* (i.e., singing) and not go beyond what it authorizes to add a second form of musical praise to the Christian religion.

Robinson defines *psallo* as follows: "to touch, to twitch, to pluck ... In Sept. and N.T. to sing, to chant, pp. as accompanying stringed instruments."[9]

Sophocles' definition is "to chant, sing religious hymns."[10]

Moulton and Milligan give the following: "properly = 'play on a harp,' but in the NT, as in Jas 5:13, = 'sing a hymn'."[11]

The German lexicographer, Bauer, defines the word to mean "to extol by singing praises, to sing praises."[12]

The Bauer lexicon as translated into English by Arndt and Gingrich offers this definition: "sing (to the accompaniment of a harp), sing praise."[13]

---

[9]Edward Robinson, *Greek and English Lexicon of the New Testament*, 1836 ed., s.v. *"psallo."*

[10]E. A. Sophocles, *Greek Lexicon of the Roman and Byzantine Periods*, 1870 ed., s.v. *"psallo."*

[11]James Hope Moulton and George Milligan, *The Vocabulary of the Greek Testament*, 1930 ed., s.v. *"psallo."*

[12]Walter Bauer, *Griechisch-Deutsches Worterbuch zu den Schriften des Neuen Testaments und der ubrigen urchristlichen Literatur*, 1952 ed., s.v. *"psallo."*

[13]Walter Bauer, *A Greek-English Lexicon of the New Testament and Other Early Christian Literature*, trans.

The monumental *Theological Dictionary of the New Testament* discusses the musical vocabulary of the early Christians and says: "*Ado.* 'To sing.' ... 'To sing of' ... There is no distinction from *psallein* in Eph. 5:19."[14]

Finally, the *New International Dictionary of New Testament Theology* says the following about the word "psalm": "In the NT two basic meanings can be ascertained. (1) *psalmos* stands for the Psalms of the OT; or the so-called *Kethubim,* 'The Writings' ... (b) More generally *psalmos* means a hymn of praise, and *psallo,* to sing a spiritual or sacred song."[15]

The correct meaning of any Greek word must be determined from its usage in context, and no lexicon is infallible in its examination of such usage. This is to say that merely pointing to a lexicon which contains a definition in agreement with one's position on a matter is not enough to settle it conclusively. All lexicographers are hu-

---

[14]Gerhard Kittel, ed., *Theological Dictionary of the New Testament,* 1964 ed., s.v. *"ado,"* by Schlier.

[15]Colin Brown, ed., *New International Dictionary of New Testament Theology,* 1978 ed., s.v. *"psalmos."*

William F. Arndt and F. Wilbur Gingrich, 1957 ed., s.v. *"psallo."*

man beings and thus subject to making mistakes. Some may even be guided by their own prejudices so as to be dogmatic and biased in assigning meanings to words. With these few observations in mind, let us examine the sources which have just been cited.[16]

First, seven of the nine lexicons or theological dictionaries already cited (Newman, Grimm-Thayer, Sophocles, Moulton-Milligan, Bauer, *TDNT,* and *NIDNTT*)support the contention that the meaning of *psallo* in the New Testament is "sing."

Second, several of the lexicons and dictionaries call attention to the fact that *psallo* has undergone significant change in the course of its history of use. In its earliest period of use in classical Greek, the word referred to plucking or twanging of any kind. It was used of pulling hair out of one's head, an archer twanging his bowstring, a carpenter twitching a chalkline, etc. Later, in the Septuagint especially, the word

---

[16]Because the controversy focuses on this word, only *psallo* will be studied in any detail. Other relevant Greek words pertaining to music in the New Testament will be omitted except for occasional incidental references.

came to refer to the twanging of strings associated with playing musical instruments such as the harp. From the sound made by playing on a harp, the word next came to be used of the song being sung to the harp. Finally, in its Jewish and Christian usage, both the noun and the verb lost the notion of instruments altogether. The noun (*psalmos*) came to refer to the Old Testament Psalms and other poetic compositions similar in form to them; the verb (*psallo*) denoted the recitation of such compositions by speaking or singing with the human voice.

In its article on *psallo,* the *Theological Dictionary of the New Testament* traces the word's history through four periods: The Greek Sphere (i.e., Greek usage uninfluenced by Jewish-Christian writings), The Old Testament and Judaism, The New Testament, and The Early Church. It is interesting to note that in discussing the second period, the writer notes that a shift of meaning has begun to occur. Although most of the Septuagint passages using *psallo* refer to playing instruments, some do not. Thus the observation: "Hence one must take into account a shift of meaning in the LXX in other passages in which the idea of playing is not evident."[17] Then, in discussing the New Testament period, Delling writes: "The literal sense 'by or with the playing of strings,' still found in the LXX, is now employed figuratively. There is nothing to suggest that *psalmos* and *hymnos* relate to texts of different genres."[18]

If one should think it strange that a word would completely change its meaning in the course of its historical development, he might consider an example in our own English language. Our word "lyric" derives from a musical instrument (i.e., lyre) but now refers to the words of a song as opposed to its melody.

Third, the two lexicons which indicate that *psallo* involves instrumental accompaniment (Robinson and Bauer-Arndt-Gingrich) can be shown to be advancing a biased opinion without supporting evidence.[19]

---

[17]*TDNT*, s.v. "*hymnos, hymneo, psallo, psalmos*," p. 494.

[18]Ibid., p. 499.

[19]An effort is made by Bro. Burgess to include Grimm-Wilke-Thayer among the lexicons favorable to instrumentation in defining *psallo*. Cf. Burgess, *Documents*, p. 28. He argues that Thayer gives his view that *psallo* includes instrumental music in a note under *hymnos* on synonymous terms. Close examination reveals that the note is a

Robinson is a dogmatic source who does not hesitate to claim more than the evidence allows when such claims are necessary to defend a denominational practice. In support of this contention, here are the comments of the same source on *baptizo:* "it would seem to have expressed not always simply immersion, but the more general idea of ablution or affusion."[20] The assertion concerning *psallo* is as trustworthy as the one on *baptizo.*

But what of the Bauer-Arndt-Gingrich lexicon? Is it not a scholarly tool held in high regard generally? Yes, and for that reason it is difficult to understand why such a mistake was made in the work. But that a mistake was made is undeniable, for the lexicon in question is a trans-

---

[20]Robinson, *Lexicon,* s.v. *"baptizo."*

---

further explanation of the Old Testament significance of the term rather than a modification of his definition. Furthermore, Thayer explicitly says in his Preface that "the frequent reference, in the discussion of synonymous terms, to the distinctions holding in classical usage ... must not be regarded as designed to modify the definitions given in the several articles. On the contrary, the exposition of classic usage is often intended merely to serve as a standard of comparison by which the direction and degree of a word's change in meaning can be measured." Grimm-Wilke-Thayer, *Lexicon,* p. vii.

lation of the original German work of Bauer. And the English translation produced by Arndt and Gingrich differs from the German original at this point.

The German source, already cited above, gives no hint of instrumental accompaniment in the word and defines *psallo* in this manner: "to extol by singing praises, to sing praises." Arndt and Gingrich did not translate Bauer at this point but extended and modified the German lexicon. Was such a change justified?

Following the death of Dr. Arndt, publishers of the English version of the Bauer lexicon contracted with Dr. Frederick Danker to work with Dr. Gingrich on possible revisions of the lexicon in question. Upon learning that such a revision was in prospect, Dr. Hugo McCord corresponded with Dr. Danker as follows:

Dr. Frederick W. Danker
Concordia Theological Seminary
St. Louis, Missouri

Dear Dr. Danker:

Your book, *Multi-Purpose Tool,* has been of great help to me.

Continually I stand amazed at the scholarship in the Arndt-Gingrich lexicon. It is my understanding that under the direction of Dr. Gingrich you are now revising that lexicon. On the word *psallo,* since Thayer, Green, Abbott-Smith, etc., limit the New Testament meaning to sing praises, I would appreciate the reasoning that brought Doctors Arndt and Gingrich to insert "to the accompaniment of the harp" in relationship to Romans 15:19; Ephesians 5:19; and I Corinthians 14:15. Further, why is the phrase excluded in relationship to James 5:13.

With all good wishes, I remain

Very truly yours,
Hugo McCord[21]

Dr. Danker replied as follows:

Dr. Hugo McCord
Oklahoma Christian College
Oklahoma City 11, Oklahoma

Dear Dr. McCord:

It was so kind of you to take the time to make your inquiry regarding the word *psallo.* I see by comparison with Bauer's first edition that the editors of A.-G. have incorporated the obvious Old Testament meaning into the metaphorical usage of the New Testament. Bauer did not make this mistake, and we will be sure to correct it in the revision. I doubt whether the archaeologists can establish the use of the harp in early Christian services.

We shall be thankful for any further corrections or

---

[21]Dr. Hugo McCord to Dr. Frederick W. Danker, 28 September 1962. A photocopy of this and related correspondence is in my possession at the courtesy of Dr. McCord.

improvements you may be able to suggest for our lexicon. The same would apply to *Multipurpose Tools for Bible Study*.

Gratefully and faithfully yours,
Frederick W. Danker[22]

In this correspondence, Dr. Danker acknowledges two significant points. First, he checked the English translation against Bauer's German original and noted that the latter had been altered in the course of translation. His speculation was that the "obvious Old Testament meaning" of *psallo* as used in the Septuagint (LXX) had been incorporated into the "metaphorical usage of the New Testament." Second, he indicated quite clearly that he regarded such a definition of the word in its New Testament context as a "mistake" in need of correction.

The outcome of the revision process reflects an appropriate change in the second edition of the lexicon. The *psallo* entry is reproduced here in full:

psallo fut. *psalo* (Aeschyl. +; inscr., LXX; Jos., Ant. 11, 67; 12, 349) in our lit., in accordance w. OT usage, sing, sing praise w. dat. of the one for whom the praise is intended *to onomati sou psalo*

---

[22]Dr. Frederick W. Danker to Dr. Hugo McCord, 2 October 1962.

Ro 15:9 (Ps 17:50). *to kurio* Eph 5:19; in this pass. a second dat. is added *to kardia humon* in or with your heart(s); here it is found with *ado* (as Ps 26:6; 32:3; 56:8), and the question arises whether a contrast betw. the two words is intended. The original mng. of *ps.* was 'pluck', 'play' (a stringed instrument); this persisted at least to the time of Lucian (cf. Parasite 17). In the LXX *ps.* freq. means 'sing', whether to the accompaniment of a harp or (as usually) not (Ps 7:18; 9:12; 107:4 al.). This process continued until *ps.* in Mod. Gk. means 'sing' exclusively; cf. *psaltes* = singer, chanter, w. no ref. to instrumental accompaniment. Although the NT does not voice opposition to instrumental music, in view of Christian resistance to mystery cults, as well as Pharisaic aversion to musical instruments in worship (s. EWerner, art. 'Music', IDB 3, 466-9), it is likely that some such sense as make melody is best here. Those who favor ; sqplay' (e.g., L-S-J; ASouter, Pocket Lexicon, '20; JMoffatt, transl. '13) may be relying too much on the earliest mng. of *psallo*. B 6:16 (cf. Ps 107:4). *ps. to pneumati* and in contrast to that *ps. to noi* sing praise in spiritual ecstasy and in full possession of one's mental faculties 1 Cor 14:15. Abs. sing praise Js 5:13. WSSmith, Musical Aspects of the NT, '62, M-M.[23]

---

[23]Walter Bauer, *A Greek-English Lexicon of the New Testament and Other Early Christian Literature,* 2nd ed., trans. William F. Arndt and F. Wilbur Gingrich, 2nd ed. revised and augmented by F. Wilbur Gingrich and Frederick W. Danker (Chicago: University of Chicago Press, 1979), s.v. *"psallo."*

Fourth, the evidence of history demonstrates that no lexicographer is justified in defining *psallo* so as to include instrumental music in the life of the first-century church. Words, after all, do not derive meaning by virtue of lexicons or authorities writing about them. Their meaning comes from usage in context. Since some of the historical evidence relevant to the definition of the word in question will be presented in the next chapter, further comment on this point will be withheld here.

Commentators

It is interesting to note the large number of commentators who are members of denominations which use instrumental music but who, nevertheless, acknowlege that the word *psallo* has no signification of instrumental accompaniment in its New Testament usage.

> This verb [*psallo*] meant primarily to touch or strike a chord, to twang the strings, and hence it is used absolutely as meaning to play the harp, etc., and in LXX to play on some stringed instrument, and also to sing to the music of the harp, often in honor of God. ... In the N.T. the same verb is used of singing of hymns, of celebrating the praise of God, Rom. xv. 9; 1 Cor. xiv. 15; Ephes. v. 19 (cf. LXX, Judg. v. 3).[24]

> *Psallo* originally meant playing on a stringed instrument; then singing to the harp or lyre; finally, singing without accompaniment, especially singing praise ...[25]

> A psalm was originally a song accompanied by a

---

[24]R. J. Knowling, *The Epistle of St. James,* 3rd ed., Westiminster Commentaries (London: Methuen and Co. Ltd., 1922), p. 137.

[25]Archibald Robertson and Alfred Plummer, *A Critical and Exegetical Commentary on the First Epistle of St. Paul to the Corinthians,* International Critical Commentary (Edinburgh: T. & T. Clark, 1914), p. 312.

stringed instrument. See on 1 Cor. 14:15. The idea of accompaniment passed away in usage, and the psalm, in New-Testament phraseology, is an Old-Testament psalm, or a composition having that character.[26]

The verb used here (*psalleto*) means, first, to twang the strings of a harp or some other musical instrument, then, to sing to the accompaniment of the harp, and then, simply to sing the praises of God in song.[27]

It is unlikely that the *psalmoi* and *hymnoi* and *odai pneumatikai* should be confined to three types of composition found in the OT Psalter – *mismorim*, *tehillim* and *shirim* respectively. Nor should the etymological force of the terms be pressed, as though *psalmos* inevitably meant a song sung to the accompaniment of a stringed instrument (psaltery or lute), the strings of which were plucked by the hand. While such plucking of the strings is the original sense of *psallo* (found in the parallel passage in Eph. 5:19), it is used in NT with the meaning 'to sing psalms' (1 Cor. 14:15; Jas. 5:13; so too, probably, in the LXX quotation in Rom. 15:9).[28]

---

[26]Marvin R. Vincent, *Word Studies in the New Testament*, Vol. III (Grand Rapids: Wm. B. Eerdmans Pub. Co., 1946), pp. 269-70.

[27]Alexander Ross, *The Epistles of James and John*, New International Commentary (Grand Rapids: Wm. B. Eerdmans Pub. Co., 1954), p. 98n.

[28]E. K. Simpson and F. F. Bruce, *Commentary on the Epistles to the Ephesians and the Colossians*, New International Commentary (Grand Rapids: Wm. B. Eerdmans Publ. Co., 1957), p. 284n.

While there are allusions made to certain instruments (for example, the harp or lyre, the pipe, the cymbal, the trumpet – and possibly the 'noisy gong' of 1 Corinthians xiii, 1), there is no certainty that any of these were actually used. The balance of probability is against such a use.[29]

M. C. Kurfees

With regard to the linguistic materials relevant to *psallo*, those of us who have followed his day owe a great debt of gratitude to the late M. C. Kurfees and the work he did on this question in the early part of the twentieth century.[30] However, Bro. Kurfees made a mistake

---

[29]Ralph P. Martin, *Worship in the Early Church* (Grand Rapids: William B. Eerdmans Pub. Co., 1974), p. 134. Dr. Martin is even more emphatic in personal correspondence where he writes: "My understanding is that the verb [*psallo*] does not have reference to the playing of musical instruments such as are referred to in, for example, Revelation 5:8. The verb relates more specifically to the exercise of vocal singing, though to be sure, if one wishes to give to the verb its precise definition, it would be 'to sing to the accompaniment of a harp.' However, in the references such as Romans 15:9; 1 Corinthians 14:15; and James 5:13, it is clear that the singing of praise is to be understood simply as the exercise of the human voice." Dr. Ralph Martin to Rubel Shelly, 13 November 1975.

[30]M. C. Kurfees, *Instrumental Music in the Worship, or the Greek Verb Psallo Philologically and Historically*

which modern students, with additional research tools, must avoid. He claimed more than the evidence will allow when he wrote

> ... the Greek word *psallo* once meant to pluck the hair, twang the bowstring, twitch a carpenter's line, and to touch the chords of a musical instrument, but had entirely lost all of these meanings before the beginning of the New Testament period, and that, therefore, the word is never used in the New Testament nor in contemporaneous literature in any of these senses. At this time, it not only meant to sing, but that is the only sense in which it was used, all the other meanings having entirely disappeared.[31]

It is not correct to say that *psallo* had lost the meaning "to play the harp" in all "contemporaneous literature" to the New Testament. It claims too much to say that there are no instances of *psallo* with its classical meaning in literature from the same general period as the New Testament. Thus Tom Burgess is able to point to several references in writers such as Strabo, Josephus, Lucian, and others where *psallo* seems clearly to be used with its meaning "play the

---

[31]Ibid., pp. 44-45.

Examined (Nashville, TN: Gospel Advocate Pub. Co., 1911.

harp."[32] Moulton and Milligan cite a second-century A.D. inscription where *psalmos* is used to specify a song sung to a harp being played by the fingers.

The case for a cappella music which has been made in this book avoids the mistake made by Kurfees by virtue of a clear distinction between *classical* Greek vocabulary and *Judeo-Christian* Greek vocabulary.[33] My claim has been

---

[32]Burgess, *Documents,* pp. 97-114. The alleged instances where he quotes Christian writers in favor of instrumental music will be noted in some detail in the next chapter.

[33]Kurfees appears to make a concession on this point in an article he wrote several years after the publication of his book. "I have conceded and do now concede that there is in Ephesians 5:19 an allusion to and a play upon the original meaning of *psallo,* but that the same passage distinctly and specifically names the 'heart' as the *instrument* on which the *psalloing* is done." This position was used generally in debate by such men as N. B. Hardeman and was an effective (and accurate) concession to the metaphorical meaning which survives in the word in its New Testament use. In the same article, Kurfees goes on to indicate his awareness of the distinction between classical and koine Greek which was not made explicit in the earlier book. He writes: "The leading mistake in the Payne book and in other discussions of the music question is the assumption that the ancient and classical meaning of *psallo* was transferred to the New Testament. This is

restricted to the usage of *psallo* and *psalmos* in their Jewish and Christian contexts. In classical Greek (e.g., the writers and inscription just mentioned) the words continued to be used to signify the use of instruments.[34] In the koine Greek of first-century Jews and Christians, the words were used without the signification of instruments.

---

[34]Although Josephus was Jewish, he rejected his Jewish allegiance in the crisis of the Jewish war with Rome, proclaimed his faith in Vespasian as Messiah, and was rejected by his own people as a traitor. He became a writer of Jewish antiquities for Roman audiences and wrote for them in Hellenistic style and vocabulary.

---

not true. The assumption is utterly groundless, and the English reader, who does not know a word of the original Greek, can learn this fact by reading its English translation both in the common version and in the revised version. The renowned scholars who made these two versions correctly understood that, in New Testament times, *psallo* was the equivalent of the modern English word 'sing' and they so translated it. No advocate of the instrumental music cause has ever been able to break the force of this fact. It stands as a Gibraltar of strength in defense of the position that vocal music, and not instrumental, is the music with which the New Testament authorizes men to praise God. Christians should be content to stand on this safe and solid ground." M. C. Kurfees, "What is Authorized by Psallo in Ephesians 5:19," *Gospel Advocate* (Sept. 13, 1923), p. 895.

This distinction between classical and New Testament Greek is not a forced distinction conjured up to fit the case being argued here. It is recognized universally among scholars of the language.

> The earliest Christian literature ... is made up of a number of writings which were composed in the Greek language. It is not the Greek of more ancient times, least of all that of the Golden Age of Athens which is now taught in the institutions of higher learning and occupies the most prominent place in the dictionaries used in them. A comparison reveals, on the contrary, differences in phonology and morphology, in syntax and style, and, not least of all, in the vocabulary as well.[35]

It has already been pointed out that the major articles in *TDNT* are divided into four sections in recognition of the distinction: (1) the word in classical context, (2) the Old Testament (i.e., LXX) usage, (3) the New Testament use, and (4) the use of the word in the church fathers.

The word *ekklesia* is a suitable and clear example of how words are used differently in the New Testament from their general use in classical vocabulary. The ordinary meaning of the word in the Greek language of the New Testa-

---

[35]Bauer, Arndt, Gingrich, and Danker, *Lexicon*, p. xi.

ment era was "assembly," and the word is even used in this common sense at Acts 19:39. In its special meaning in the New Testament vocabulary, however, *ekklesia* is the word translated "church." In the former case the word can refer to an assembly of any type; in the latter it refers to a very special group of people, the redeemed.

The interesting thing is that the same mistake made by Kurfees is typically made by those who defend instrumental music as worship. Burgess, for example, produces his evidences on behalf of *psallo* including instruments by citing dictionaries and teachers of classical Greek. Such "evidence" is irrelevant to the study of the word in the New Testament. It is admitted that *psallo* referred to instrumentation in classical Greek. The issue which must be faced is its meaning in Jewish and Christian contexts at the time of Christ and the apostles.

It is therefore correct to admit that Kurfees claimed too much in his early work on this subject. It is incorrect, however, to say that this admits the claim of some that *psallo* in the New Testament means to sing with instruments.

Conclusion

This chapter has given proof that the New Testament usage of *psallo* does not entail singing to the accompaniment of instruments. It has been shown that lexicographers and commentators who have no "anti-instrument bias" acknowledge that *psallo* in the New Testament means simply "sing, sing praise." In the next chapter, we shall examine historical data which undergirds this definition.

The Historical Evidence

When one undertakes a study of any biblical topic, it is important to put the matter into its total historical context. For example, in studying New Testament baptism, one should pay attention both to its Jewish antecedents (i.e., ablutions required in the Law, proselyte baptism, and the baptism of John) and the practice of baptism among Christians of the second and third centuries (i.e., the so-called "church fathers"). The fact that historical investigation reveals baptism to have been performed always by immersion in the period immediately surrounding the first century is part of the evidence which (1) demands that the Greek word *baptizo* be understood to refer to the action of submerging an object or person in an element and (2) compels us to insist on immersion as the only acceptable form of New Testament baptism. In such a situation, neither the church fathers nor history is our authority for what we teach or practice. It is simply that the evidence from such sources has assisted us in interpreting the New Testament with confidence. Scripture remains our sole authority, but historical evidence has assisted us in understanding the requirement of the Word of God.

One is in precisely the same situation with regard to a study of the music of the early church. If historical evidence demonstrates that the music of the early church was unaccompanied singing, one is unjustified in claiming that *psallo* signifies instrumentation or that we can use mechanical instruments in our worship of God today and claim to be following the example of the earliest disciples of Christ.

The testimony of history is altogether against the practice of instrumental music in the church of the New Testament era.

Jewish Background

Historians generally begin any discussion of music in the Christian religion by pointing to its Jewish backgrounds.

It is a generally accepted fact that Jewish worship in New Testament times, both of Palestinian Jews and Jews of the Dispersion, centered around the synagogue. In these synagogues, instrumental music was not employed. Although a variety of instruments played by professional musicians were used in the temple service until its destruction in A.D. 70, those instruments were not only *absent* but were also *rejected as unsuitable* for the type of worship being conducted at the synagogue.

According to 1 Chronicles 23:5, 4,000 musicians were appointed to praise Yahweh with instruments. The instruments would have been cymbals, harps, and psalteries. Trumpets were also employed but were apparently played only by the priests in connection with certain rituals. As large a figure as 4,000 is to us, it pales beside the numbers given by Josephus. If he is taken as an accurate source on the matter, Solomon provided the temple with 40,000 psalteries and harps and 200,000 trumpets.[1]

With a background of what could be legitimately called orchestral music at the temple, it is somewhat surprising to take note of the attitude of the synagogue. An eminent Jewish source, observes:

> Jingling, banging, and rattling accompanied heathen cults, and the frenzying shawms of a dozen ecstatic rites intoxicated the masses. Amid this euphoric farewell feast of a dying civilization, the voices of nonconformists were emerging from places of Jewish and early Christian worship; Philo of Alexandria had already emphasized the ethical qualities of music, spurning the 'effeminate' art of his Gentile surroundings. Similarly, early synagogue song intentionally foregoes artistic perfection, renounces the playing of instruments, and attaches itself entirely to 'the word' – the text of the Bible.[2]

The significance of this information lies in the fact that the worship of the early church was very similar in pattern and purpose to that of the synagogue as opposed to the temple.

---

[1] Josephus *Antiquities* 8. 3. 8.

[2] *Encyclopaedia Judaica,* 1971 ed., s.v. "Music."

With particular reference to music, "all evidence points to the chant and music of the primitive church as practically identical with the customs and traditions of the synagogue."[3]

Gerhard Delling, a German scholar regarded as one of the leading authorities on the subject of first-century worship, has documented the fact that Jews of the period had come to use the terms "psalm," "hymn," and "song" (cf. Eph.5:19; Col.3:16) interchangeably and points out that the psalms were sung in the synagogues without instrumental accompaniment. He writes: "In the New Testament there is nowhere any emphasis laid on the musical form of the hymns; and in particular none on instrumental accompaniment (whereas this is significant in paganism)."[4]

Church History

Leaving the subject of Jewish backgrounds

---

[3]*Interpreter's Dictionary of the Bible,* 1962 ed., s.v. "Music."

[4]Gerhard Delling, *Worship in the New Testament,* trans. Percy Scott (Philadelphia: Westminster Press, 1962), p. 86.

and coming directly to the matter of church history, any number of historians can be cited to substantiate the claim that instrumental music was not connected with the worship of the early church. Only a few representative quotations from sources reflecting various perspectives will be given here.

The following statements are made not by theologians but writers treating the history of music:

> In the early Christian Church there was, however, a strong feeling against the use of instruments in divine worship. Some have thought to account for this by the secrecy which the Christians had to adopt for their gatherings for worship, on account of the persecution to which they were exposed. But if that had been the reason, it would have silenced the voice of song as well. Yet in spite of the persecution which made the infant Church hide her head 'mid ignominy, death, and tombs,' vocal music seems to have been a regular part of the ritual.[5]

> The development of Western music was decisively influenced by the exclusion of musical instruments from the early Christian Church.[6]

---

[5]George W. Stewart, *Music in Church Worship* (London: Hodder and Stoughton, Ltd., 1926), p. 214.

[6]Paul Henry Lang, *Music in Western Civilization* (New York: W. W. Norton and Co. Inc., 1941), p. 54.

The early Christians refused to have anything to do with the instrumental music which they might have inherited from the ancient world. By limiting their musical tradition, which much later was to be the matrix out of which modern music grew, to choral music, they unconsciously made more difficult the process by which an independent self-sufficient musical art could develop. In other words, music was destined to be bound to language for a good many centuries.[7]

Only singing, however, and no playing of instruments, was permitted in the early Christian Church.[8]

The primitive Christian community held the same view, as we know from apostolic and post-apostolic literature: instrumental music was thought unfit for religious services; the Christian sources are quite outspoken in their condemnation of instrumental performances. Originally, only song was considered worthy of direct approach to the Divinity.[9]

All ancient Christian music was vocal. 'We need one instrument: the peaceful word of adoration, not harps or drums or pipes or trumpets,' said St. Clement of Alexandria around 200 A.D.[10]

---

[7]Theodore M. Finney, *A History of Music,* rev. ed. (New York: Harcourt, Brace and Company, 1947), p. 43.

[8]Hugo Leichtentritt, *Music, History and Ideas* (Cambridge, MA: Harvard University Press, 1947), p. 34.

[9]Eric Werner, "The Music of Post-Biblical Judaism," in *The New Oxford History of Music,* Vol. 1, ed. Egon Wellesz (London: Oxford University Press, 1957), p. 315.

[10]Curt Sachs, *Our Musical Heritage,* 2nd ed. (Englewood-Cliffs: Prentice-Hall, Inc., 1955), p. 43.

Dr. Ralph Martin, formerly of the London Bible College and later a professor at Fuller Theological Seminary, writes of New Testament worship and insists:

> There is no evidence for the use of musical instruments; and if we picture the believers as men and women drawn from the poorer strata of society and meeting clandestinely, the non-mention of instrumental music is not surprising. The 'making melody' (*psallontes:* Eph.v.19) is 'in the heart'.[11]

Of particular interest is an article in the *Catholic Encyclopedia* which states: "For almost a thousand years Gregorian chant, without any instrumental or harmonic addition, was the only music used in connexion with liturgy."[12] Later in the same article, the writer continues:

> Pius X, in his 'Motu proprio' on church music (22 November, 1903) in paragraph IV, says, 'Although the music proper to the Church is purely vocal music, music with the accompaniment of the organ is also permitted ... As the chant should always have the first place, the organ or instruments should merely sustain and never suppress it.' ... And it is recog-

---

[11]Ralph P. Martin, "Aspects of Worship in the New Testament Church," *Vox Evangelica* 2 (1963), p. 12; cf. Martin, *Worship in the Early Church* (Grand Rapids: William B. Eerdmans Pub. Co., 1974), pp. 39-52.

[12]*Catholic Encyclopedia* 1913 ed., s.v. "Musical."

nized, and in many places acted upon, that the new version of the liturgical chant, proposed to the Catholic world by Pius X, gains its full beauty and effectiveness only when sung without instrumental accompaniment of any kind.[13]

The testimony of musicologists and church historians is uniform in its force. It was not the practice of the earliest Christians to use instruments in place of or as accompaniment to their singing of praise to God.

Patristic Evidence

As to the data concerning instrumental music from the church fathers, it is uniformly negative. The most complete collection of patristic statements relative to the subject at hand is found in the doctoral dissertation of James William McKinnon, "The Church Fathers and Musical Instruments."[14] Dr. McKinnon found something less than a hundred passages which he studied

---

[13]Ibid.

[14]James William McKinnon, "The Church Fathers and Musical Instruments" (Ph. D. dissertation, Columbia University, 1965).

critically in the course of his research. A summary of his findings is as follows:

> The Fathers of the early Church were virtually unanimous in their hostility toward musical instruments....
>
> Early Christianity inherited its musical practices and attitudes from Judaism, especially from the Synagogue. Unlike the Temple the Synagogue employed no instruments in its services. The absence of instruments did not result from antagonism toward instruments, whether the instruments of the Temple or of the Hellenistic cults, but from the simple fact that instruments had no function in the unique service of the Synagogue. The Synagogue, with its readings from Scripture, its prayers and psalms was unlike any other cult manifestation of antiquity; it alone dispensed with the typical primitive rites such as animal sacrifice and orgiastic dancing, all of which employed musical instruments. The Synagogue's rites were absorbed into the early Christian Mass, and the vocal music of the Synagogue, especially psalmody, was fostered by Christians with considerable enthusiasm.
>
> The polemic against musical instruments must be distinguished from this positive fostering of unaccompanied song. The polemic did not develop until the third and fourth centuries, and therefore came into existence long after the basic Christian musical practices and attitudes had been established....
>
> One arrives then at two distinct yet related conclusions. There is the fact that early Christian music was vocal and there is the patristic polemic against

instruments. The two are related in that an analysis of the polemic confirms the fact.[15]

Another interesting statement by McKinnon which is of importance to the issues at stake in this book is this one:

> The patristic attitude was virtually monolithic, even though it was shared by men of diverse temperament and different regional backgrounds, and even though it extended over a span of at least two centuries of accelerated development for the Church. That there were not widespread exceptions to the general position defies historical credibility. Accordingly many musicologists, while acknowledging that early Church music was predominately vocal, have tried to produce evidence that instruments were employed in the liturgy at various times and places. The result of such attempts has been a history of misinterpretations and mistranslations.[16]

Many writers who admit that instrumental music was not a part of the worship of the first-century church insist its absence was merely a cultural phenomenon rather than a doctrinal or theological matter.[17] We are asked to believe that

---

[15]Ibid., pp. 1-2.

[16]Ibid., p. 261.

[17]A case in point is Robert P. Donalson, "Music in Worship: Ritual Practice or Spiritual Principle," *Mission* (March 1970), pp. 269-276.

early Christians "excluded [instruments] not so much because of some theological horror but simply because they could not maintain a truly spiritual frame of mind in the presence of instruments which had so many pagan connotations."[18]

Although this is a commonly offered explanation for the rejection of instrumental music by early Christians, it appears inadequate for several reasons. First, the earliest Christians were all Jews who had a rich and varied musical heritage through the temple. They would not have thought of musical instruments in terms of their "pagan connotations" but in terms of the worship of God at Jerusalem. Second, Mc-Kinnon has already been quoted concerning synagogue worship to the effect that the lack of instruments "did not result from antagonism towards instruments ... but from the simple fact that instruments had no function in the unique service of the Synagogue." The Jewish synagogue was concerned primarily with the instruction of its adherents in the Word of God. Instrumental music did not contribute to this end

---

[18]Ibid., p. 276.

and was thus rejected for this reason. A music historian writes:

> The basic proposition in the philosophy of the Church Fathers was that music is the servant of religion. Only that music is good which, without obtruding its own charms, opens the mind to Christian teachings and disposes the soul to holy thoughts. Music without words cannot do this; hence instrumental music was excluded from public worship, though the faithful were allowed to use a lyre to accompany the singing of hymns and psalms in their homes and on informal occasions.[19]

Third, the rejection of instruments from the worship of the church was also due to its incompatibility with the nature of that worship. "Let the word of Christ dwell in you richly; in all wisdom teaching and admonishing one another with psalms and hymns and spiritual songs, singing with grace in your hearts unto God" (Col. 3:16). The music envisioned in this text was to contribute the establishment of the "word of Christ" in the heart of the worshipper. In fact, the worship offered by a child of God is always to be "spiritual" or "of the reason" (cf.

---

[19]Donald Jay Grout, *A History of Western Music* (New York: W. W. Norton & Company, Inc., 1960), p. 31.

Rom. 12:1f; 1 Pet. 2:2ff). Commenting on this same point, J. W. Roberts has said:

> Furthermore, in 1 Corinthians 12-14 Paul's entire discussion of the questions rising out of the public worship 'when the whole church comes together' (1 Corinthians 14:26) is that this principle of rational activity which leads to the edification of the whole church on the principle that love is to be the basis of regulation of activity: 'Let all things be done unto edification' ... Nor is it lacking in relevance to point out that Paul's very illustration of how useless something may be which cannot be understood is that of 'a lifeless instrument, such as the flute or the harp' which does not give a distinct sound. ... What does not contribute to 'edification' is to be rejected.[20]

The conclusion from all this information is compelling. Whether viewed from its antecedents in Judaism, its successors of the sub-apostolic era, or biblical and other historical data concerning the first-century church, the practice of the early church involved singing as its means of musical praise to God. Instrumental music came much later as a medieval addition by the Roman Catholic Church.

---

[20]J. W. Roberts, "Is the Reason for Accepting or Rejecting Instrumental Music Sociological – Or is it Theological?" *Mission* (March 1970): p. 280.

Early Christians Favoring Instruments?

In attempting to offset the historical and patristic data concerning instrumental music, some writers have alleged that there is no uniformity of opposition to instrumental music as worship among the church fathers. They have even alleged to find statements of approbation for instrumental music as worship.

> Some ancient writers were in favor of using instruments in connection with worship. Clement of Alexandria, A.D. 190, both favored and opposed. He prohibited flutes, trumpets, drums, and the sistrum, and 'Egyptian clapping of hands.' ... Clement made a specific exception in the case of the harp, 'the instrument of David,' as 'innocent and permissible' for Christian services.[21]

It is clearly a mistake to cite this statement from Clement so as to indicate that he approved instruments in Christian worship. The section of his preserved writing in question is from *The Instructor* (2. 4.) and has nothing to do with

---

[21]Dwaine Dunning, "New Thoughts on an Old Problem," *Christian Standard* (Feb. 19, 1966), p. 121. Essentially the same point is made concerning Clement in Burgess, *Documents,* pp. 105-109.

"Christian services." Chapter IV is explicitly titled "How to Conduct Ourselves at Feasts" and describes the excesses of pagan revelry witnessed at public festivals. Clement denounces the music found in such situations as leading to lust and license; the one exception he makes is for the harp or lyre. But notice that its use is to be tolerated at a public banquet rather than at a Christian love feast or worship context.

So opposed were the church fathers to instrumental music that it was their general practice to forbid and inveigh against them in every setting. Clement is notable for allowing one instrument (i.e., the harp) in one setting (i.e., a feast). No other early church father dissents from a blanket condemnation of instruments of all sorts by Christians for either worship or public use.

Theodoret, bishop of Cyrrhus in Syria, wrote:

Question: If songs were invented by unbelievers to seduce men, but were allowed to those under the law on account of their childish state, why do those who have received the perfect teaching of grace in their churches still use songs, just like the children under the law?

Answer: It is not simple singing that belongs to the childish state, but singing with lifeless instruments, with dancing, and with clappers. Hence the use of such instruments and the others that belong to the childish state is excluded from the singing in the churches, and simple singing is left.[22]

So he also allowed the use of instrumental music, not that he was delighted by the harmony, but that he might little by little end the deception of the idols.[23]

Niceta, bishop of Remesiana in what is today Yugoslavia, contrasts the worship under two different covenants and says:

It is time to turn to the New Testament to confirm what is said in the Old, and, particularly, to point out that the office of psalmody is not to be considered abolished merely because many other observances of the Old Law have fallen into desuetude. Only the corporal institutions have been rejected, like circumcision, the sabbath, sacrifices, discrimination in foods. So, too, the trumpets, harps, cymbals and timbrels. For the sound of these we now have a better substitute in the music from the mouths of men.[24]

John Crysostom, known as the greatest preacher of the Greek church and bishop of Constantinople, wrote:

---

[22]*Questions and Answers for the Orthodox*, Q. 107. Note: This and the three following quotations are cited from translations used by Ferguson, *A Cappella Music*, (Abilene, TX: Biblical Research Press, 1972), pp. 53-55.

[23]*On the Healing of Greek Afflictions* 7:16.

[24]*On the Utility of Hymn Singing*.

Many people take the mention of these instruments allegorically and say that the timbrel required the putting to death of our flesh, and that the psaltery requires us to look up to heaven (for this instrument resounds from above, not from below like the lyre). But I would say this, that in olden times they were thus led by these instruments because of the dullness of their understanding and their recent deliverance from idols. Just as God allowed animal sacrifices, so also he let them have these instruments, condescending to help their weakness.[25]

Otherwise any favorable mention of instruments by these writers is either with reference to their use in pre-Christian times by the Jews or is in connection with allegorical interpretation of Old Testament musical texts wherein an instrument or its parts are held to represent parts of the human body.[26]

Later Church History

Of far less importance for establishing early Christian practice, yet interesting nonetheless, is the attitude toward instrumental music over the years of church history.

---

[25]*On Psalms* 149:2.

[26]An excellent analysis of references of this sort is found in Ferguson, *A Cappella Music,* pp. 47-83.

We are unsure about the date of introduction of instruments into worship contexts. The Greek (Eastern) Church, of course, has never tolerated instrumental music of any sort in its services. The Latin (Roman Catholic) Church had begun using instruments fairly widely by the tenth century, but its origin there is uncertain. Some date it by the gift of an organ to King Pepin in 757 and others trace it at least to Vitalian I in the mid-seventh century.

In connection with the Protestant Reformation, instruments were generally opposed as a "popish addition" to the New Testament precedent for the church and abandoned. Luther called the organ an ensign of Baal, and Knox referred to it as a "kist (i.e., chest) of whistles."

Like most religious reformers, Calvin relied on song by the people, and discourages musical instruments, which he compared to childish toys which ought to be put away in manhood. So deeply did his teaching sink into the Genevans, that three years after his death they melted down the pipes of the organ in his church, to form flagons for the communion.

And his principles were adopted widely in Britain.[27]

So thoroughly did the English sentiment come

W. T. Whitley, *Congregational Hymn-Singing* (London: J. M. Dent & Sons Ltd., 1933), p. 58.

to oppose instrumental music in worship contexts that Parliament ordered all organs removed from churches and chapels in May of 1644.[28] The objection was not to the use of such instruments in home or private situations but to church use. The determination seems to have been that vocal praise to the Almighty would not be overwhelmed by the music of a machine. The fear was also expressed that entertainment by paid performers could eventually replace those who desired to worship personally in song. The sentiment was argued that neither singing nor praying could be done by proxy, thus each member was to discharge his responsibility by raising his own voice to God.

When, in the nineteenth century, organs began to make their way into some of the churches around London, they were stigmatized as "Baal, the idol of the Philistines."[29] Some would leave the chapel when it was used with a hymn and return only when it fell silent to resume their worship.

The use of instrumental music in America

---

[28] Ibid., p. 83.

[29] Ibid., p. 201.

was not the norm in the early days of this country. Whether among Presbyterians, Baptists, Methodists, or other groups, strong opposition was expressed to its use. It came to be used in the nineteenth century only over much protest and at the end of heated debate.

The Puritans of New England derisively referred to organs as the "devil's bagpipes" and regarded them as too reminiscent of Rome to have any place in their worship. Yet it eventually happened that

> ... the question of organs in churches became a very live one among the colonists, and for more than a century it continued to be the center of more or less bitter controversy. When a few New England progressives hinted a desire for an organ, they were sternly suppressed by the eminent Cotton Mather, who solemnly argued that if organs were permitted, other instruments would soon follow, and then there would come dancing![30]

The first organ accepted into a New England church was set up in King's Chapel of Boston in 1714 (Church of England). The second was

---

[30]Edward S. Ninde, The Story of the American Hymn (New York: Abingdon Press, 1921), p. 95. Cf. Richard D. Dinwiddie, "Fruit Pies, Popcorn, and Music," *Christianity Today* (Nov. 23, 1984), pp. 30-32.

not installed until 1733 at Trinity Church in Newport, Rhode Island. As late as 1800, it is estimated that there were less than 20 organs in all of New England.[31]

The initiation of the use of instruments in America's City of Brotherly Love, Philadelphia, seems to have been particularly acrimonious. A Presbyterian wrote a little pamphlet in 1763 which indicated his clear disgust for "those groveling souls" who objected to instruments generally and the organ in particular. He quoted an "eminent Divine" who had allegedly told his audience that there were only

> Three Kinds of Beings that he knew of, whom God had endowed with Animal Sensation, who were not charm'd with the Harmony of Musick, and they were the Devil, a Quaker, and an Ass.[32]

He continued by saying that Presbyterians and Baptists ought to be included also by virtue of the fact that the

> ... miserable manner in which this Part of their Worship is droll'ed out, seems rather to imitate the

---

[31]Dwight Steere, *Music in Protestant Worship* (Richmond, VA: John Knox Press, 1960), p. 35.

[32]Quoted in Ninde, *American Hymn,* p. 98.

Braying of Asses, than the divine Melody so often recommended in Scripture.[33]

Literature of this sort which survives demonstrates that the instrument issue caused bitter feelings not only among churches associated with the American Restoration Movement but also earlier among religious groups generally in the United States. Perhaps only because our involvement in the controversy came late and resulted in a permanent division within the movement is it thought by some observers to be unique to us.

Ben Franklin, the restoration preacher, estimated shortly after the end of the Civil War that only 50 or so churches associated with the movement used the instrument in worship. By 1885, however, an obvious division over the issue was in evidence among brethren. In 1906 a separate census listing was made for those who did and did not use the instrument in worship.

The unfortunate division persists to this day.

---

[33]Ibid.

A
Final
Word

In this little book, I have tried to set forth a case for a cappella music as the exclusive form of musical praise appropriate to the New Testament church. I have explained why I believe the use of musical instruments as worship is a move away from the solid rock of biblical authority where souls may anchor with full confidence.

Because my convictions on this matter are so strong, I cannot but teach against the use of instruments as worship and plead with people who sincerely wish to follow the New Testament order of things to abstain from or to abandon the practice.

If an effort were to be made to introduce the instrument into a local church where I held membership or into our larger fellowship of believers, I would oppose it strenuously. If the contrary position prevailed, I would have to exit the group and forego the fellowship of worship which I believed to be unscriptural.

Having spoken so frankly in the few lines above of the depth of my feeling on this issue, I can only hope that the preceding pages have been written in a spirit appropriate to a Christian student. For while my convictions are deep, I have no right to be harsh in presenting an argument or unfair with any of the relevant facts. All parties concerned must be diligent to learn and obey the will of God. We shall all stand before the same Lord and answer to him in the Last Day.

As different ones of us continue to study this issue which divides believers, let all of us pray for God to show mercy to his children. We must constantly remind ourselves that our hope is not based on flawless theology and perfect practice; it is based on the grace of God which has been manifested in Christ Jesus.

Our Father, we pray for you to take away the errors in our understanding and the sins from our lives. Free us from suspicion and fear of one another. And as you draw us closer to yourself, let us realize that you are drawing us closer to each other in the same act.

Help us to focus our faith on Jesus and to burn with the desire to share the gospel with the world. Show us how to break down the walls which keep your children apart and cause us to be weak in our divisions. Teach us to build bridges rather than walls. Let our love for you be so great that our differences with each other will be addressed with a genuine desire for oneness in the Truth.

Father, keep us from presumptuous sin. Hold us securely in your grace. And teach us to reach out to one another with the same spirit you show in reaching out to all of us. In the name of our precious Lord, we pray. Amen.

SING HIS PRAISE!

RUBEL SHELLY

A CASE FOR A CAPPELLA MUSIC AS WORSHIP TODAY